All my faces

A poetry collection by

Jasmijn Muijser

Copyright © 2025 Jasmijn Muijser
All rights reserved.
ISBN: 9798306492339

DEDICATION

This book is for all the versions of me
who felt like they weren't loved
and couldn't breathe freely

I see you
I love you
And I'm here

AUTHOR'S NOTE

I wrote this book when I was eighteen. It is my first introduction, not only to the publishing scene- but also to writing poetry. Don't get me wrong, I have always loved writing. I wrote my first book at twelve years old and ever since then got addicted to the feeling of it. But I always wrote novels- not poetry. Not seriously at least. But that changed when the idea of *All my faces* came to me. It seemed a crazy thing to do at first, but the idea kept nagging at me, persistent like a bad cold, and so I had no choice but to listen to the muse.

After this, I spent a lot of late summer nights scribbling down poems in my notebook and then transferring them to a secret document on my laptop. Suddenly, one month later, it was there; my debut poetry book about love, girlhood, being afraid to grow up and mental illness.

All such sensitive topics that lie so closely to my heart and to who I am- not just as a poet- but as a person.

All my faces

I wrote about my experience of dealing with mental illness since my teenage years and how hard it is to deal with some days. Especially when society more often than not, only offers its comfort by telling you how difficult you are.

I wrote about the loss of loved ones and how that grief can linger even on the warmest days. I also wrote about girlhood, and how some days it can feel like an open wound. And lastly, I wrote about being afraid. To get older, to lose things and to have everything change.

Please keep in mind that this book deals with sensitive topics, such as depression, suicide, death, reflecting upon an eating disorder and grief.

That all being said; this book is a love letter to all the versions of me I've been throughout my life and all the faces I have worn.

Love,

Jaz

All my faces

Jasmijn Muijser

1 All my faces

I hope if I tear myself up
in all the right places
that I'll finally extract something worthwhile
A book I wrote, a price I won,
an ace to play at the races
I feel I run yet *never win*

Is my suffering for the world to judge?
Am I inconvenient, will they be lenient?
If they see how hard I've tried?
To be loved, to be good
Will they be fair if they knew
in silence, how many times I've died?

I can't shake this feeling
of being a doll in a glass house
Always being looked at, trapped
like a mouse, it's left me reeling
I want to feel
and if I do

All my faces

Is it even real?

Am I beyond all my faces
my masks I pick to show the world
Am I someone
or after all this time

Have I simply become a mould?

Jasmijn Muijser

2 Pull yourself together, please

I stay home from class
too often, no longer an academic weapon
God, I'm such a mess
I try so hard
to stop the bleeding,
can't handle this feeling
It leaks from my eyes
I know I can be better *but*
it's winter in my chest and
I can't escape this weather
No energy in my bed
I'm a restless little feather
Did I fall from grace?
I can't mess up my grades
Why can't I pull myself together?
I just let it happen
and my parents
don't
understand

3 Lawnmower

Somewhere inside me
there are nerves
always running,
it's a curse
I caught when I was young
now there's no air in my lungs
When I sleep I think it's over
then it rips up my chest
sits upon me so heavily
like a goddamn lawnmower

Anxiety never rests

4 I swear I've changed

I'm so afraid
of rushing into you
and you'll see me
Not for who I am
but for who I was
Because I've changed, truly

Can't you see?

5 Barrel of a gun

I'm staring
down the barrel
of a gun
that takes my childhood

Tears me
to pieces
Drowning in blood,
I seek
for a way to fix it

To stay in this place
so everything can stay the same

I don't want to let it all go

6 Ceilings

Some days
of my life
I lay in my bed
staring at the ceiling
and as the tears slip
past my eyes
and I become sadness
I think I'm the most
myself

I have *ever* been

7 Storm shelter barren ground

It's been a while
since I've written
since I have felt
the light I know
it hides within me
storm shelter, barren ground

I am a daughter
I don't know how

I'll sleep until I'm better
the seasons change, turn brighter

Why is it
that I just *never do*?

8 Please help me

I cry for my mother
like a river, little girl
In my nightmares,
my waking life
I don't want to grow older
Please help me, I'm so afraid
I just want to go back
play in the garden
with my sister and the sun
shone so bright like I did
and I wasn't so tired
please help me
I'm
so
afraid

9 All I've done

I've lost a friend
a wound I cannot mend
When I was young
I lost all hope
Can't recommend,
it is a deadly slope

And so
all I've ever done
has been in favour
of trying
to win it
back

10 Bones

My bones
buried themselves
back
into my body
afraid

of the *cold*

11 Once upon a time

Everywhere I go
I find pieces
of you
and how our lives
belonged together
once upon a time

12 Pointless hurt

In the depth
of my soul
I search for things
I know, deep down
this life
will *never*
be able
to give me

13 A girl and her bath

I'm laying here
body in the water
wondering
what version of me
I should
unbecome

14 Set in stone?

I'm so afraid
to show up differently

Ruin
the image
others have of me

When I know
deep down
I'd be so much more
free

15 Distance

I love you ~~more~~

when you're not here

16 Pain is now trendy

On the internet
they tell you
to find solace in your demons
to leave the past behind

All these gurus you pay
to give you
answers, hope, some peace of mind
To buy supplements
and distractions
when that's only a fraction
of what your heart really needs

I think
we should reconsider
this "healing" trend
and the idea we have
about pain and its dark days
Perhaps instead of
catchy promises
and a step by step paid guide

All my faces

on "how to mend"

we should listen
to our pain
slow down and accept it
let it become our compass
and our *friend*

17 Florentine

Florentine, oh Florentine
What'd you do to me?
heartbreak and misery
Your shores are so empty
Horizon still, my sun still plenty
enough time to change your mind
redirect your love, you left me behind

Last man standing
I've stranded someplace lost
heart flayed
still a little in love
and a little sanded

I'm here if you need me
No not anymore, sadly
Not after what you broke

Florentine,
I loved you so

18 Anger

Where do I leave this anger
this fury
you bestowed upon me?

Adding insult to injury
there is no medicine to cure me
For decades women have been taught
not to portray it, convey it to
silence as long as you go unheard

This curse I caught
in blood and bones
it is no fraud
I am angry, never fraught
I am a weapon, volatile dragon
They tell me I'm *just a little bird*

19 Crime scene

I want to cut myself open
just to get you out
from underneath my skin

Crimson tears are spilling
loving you was such a *thrill*
You're gone now
and I'm so angry I think I hate you
How can I?
Can I?

Amidst the smoke
your love revoked
I'm left here reeling
What was the reason?
What am I feeling?
I'm torn open, can't speak
Am I bleeding out?
I feel so weak

All my faces

I hear your name and it's like a knife
to what I knew, believed in
My whole life, all this time, and now it's gone
slipped away, bottle empty, pavement wine
The shape of my body, mapped out, red

I think I hear the sirens
too far away to save me-
you planned it all ahead

Jasmijn Muijser

20 Not anymore

Perhaps all my uneventful summers
have prepared me for something new

In the wake of you I was empty
while during us love lacked
I've now found plenty
Few caught
the strained tension
the exchange of stormy glares
pause in your step as you walked by
I'm sure if they asked you
like you always do, you made up some lie

My reputation was once so tender
so affected by public opinion
I no longer feel the need to mend her

I can't say I never loved you
I'm just glad I can say I *no longer do*

21 Judas

Judas,
this Eve you turn nineteen

Judas,
your true nature
I could never have foreseen

Judas,
from you
I'll spend my life
getting clean

22 Window

Back up,
I feel so still

Back up,
now my heart's been killed

Leave me
to the garden
where all things die

Leave me
after you watched
all my hope fly
out the window
to the wind
And
  You
    Just
        stood there

23 My mama told me so

You made me trade
my value for bittersweet
kisses, I wasn't your missus
your number one, the one you love
and keep in mind and heart
what a false start, I didn't see it then
love turned poison, that I
ingested, all this time and energy
I invested, into loving you

It was all for nothing
your lies were drugging
my judgement- I've been
forgotten, been replaced
my faith in you misplaced
although my mother warned me
from the start, I was young
and naive and
I
believed

All my faces

in

us

Would've given you my forever
Should've known you'd turn out
to be *treasonous*

24 Ballerina

I'm sitting like a worn ballerina
a puppet on your strings
Broken toy, play with me
in this hollow theatre
where no one ever wins

Rain pours down
through this shattered roof
As salty as my tears
the public pretends not to see
A little crowd's enjoyment
at the expense of my heart
the laughingstock
the it was "just a joke"
so casually
they tear me apart

I am weighed down
Tired, overextended limbs
useless, it's of no use
they took my spirit

All my faces

they melted my crown

I used to be in places
soaring, high on life
now my ambition has vanished
and I'm doing all I can to survive

How hopeless here with the rest
of once so promising children
They thought we'd go places
one of those remembered faces
Now we're faceless, sick and grey
there's a noose around our spark
a blanket around our fire
Eventually,
don't all stars dire?

I hang from the ceiling
all I can is
sway

Jasmijn Muijser

25 Slaughterhouse

Some butcher's daughter
chopped my trust to pieces
Left me to hang
flayed and freezing

Some days
I still wonder
why
She did
what she did
to me

26 I will have my orange trees

I was never your thing
Honeysuckle with thorns
I thought surely for your love
I must have been born

Silly me for assuming
that together our fates would cling
All that hope ever got me
was a heart now scorned

Spring blessed fire
you doused the flame
And for what?
To appear cooler?
To clear your name?

Why do I do this?
Thinking they're better
worthy, just like in my head
I fantasise about our stories
forgoing all worries

Jasmijn Muijser

All my faces

I pick only happy endings
my heart can't take more mending

Orange trees in the yard
Someday,
I won't be so alone

27 Moving on never leaves me indifferent

Railroad of ruined travels

connecting us by the heart

I remember your smiles

Our shared beliefs, our laughter

hopes and dreams that reached the sky

I thought time couldn't break us,

turns out it's *already passed us by*

28 Matcha

I drink my matcha
with the stars and a side of self-reflection
Saltwater freckles accompany me
like the beautiful looking girls I see
in pictures and videos
Surely if this is what they're doing
it must have the same effect on me?

29 Paper sleeves

I'm an artist
so I bleed myself out
in ink, my dreams
silver linings, childhood traumas
I wear them on paper sleeves

God forbid things will go unspoken
All my near deaths a special token
to remain a focal point
of creativity
so I can create
But what if I can't?
What will there be left of me?

Am I a shell
a worn-out performance
of thoughts that have long been spoken
Can I be something new?

All my faces

Are my words still of meaning
even if they are not shaded blue?

30 Nothing more in me

For a long time
I believed sex was about giving love to others
But life hit hard and shattered me apart
a dozen different, unfitting parts
It drained me empty

So now, will it break your heart
when I tell you
I have nothing more in me
to gift to you?

31 Sober sins

I've loved you before you were sober
and I have loved you everyday since

I only ask of you to return that effort
and not condemn me for my sins

32 Lighthouse

If I were to love you
You'd be a lighthouse to my storm
A point of origin
A way not to get lost

Can you shoulder this burden?
Can you take it
if I were
to drown?

33 Narcissus you should know

Don't drag me down there
to be with you

I am deserving of better
If you loved me enough
to outdo your own image

Narcissus, you would know
sometimes distance is better
than *toxic love*

34 Integrity

I question my integrity
my character
my purpose in this world
On separate occasions
I am someone different
a mirrorball, a dayfly
a theatre full of dolls

Who am I really?
Why can I not stay true
to this idea I have of me?
Is it my ego
my traumas
or am I just *lost?*

35 A thousand men's kisses

I crave the touch
of a thousand men's kisses

But just the touch
of a thorough, honest lover

would cure *the hunger in me*

36 Kill me gently

I drown myself in these sorrows
let the taste of salt spill my tongue
I'd ask you to kill me gently
but I have never
known your touch to be *so*

37 You

The last thing I wanted

was to be wanted

by anyone

that wasn't

you

38 Lying altar girl

Do you see me?
Or just your reflection
upon this crystallised sky
Our rotten love no longer benign

Malnourished, malevolent, your malpractices
and chastises- you act like I'm the one
who hurt you, I'm the saboteur
who made you want to die
Cry like a baby, blank sheet- so naive
have you truly no idea what you've done?

How could you, why would you-
do what you did?
Rip up my heart and feast upon me like prey
Dish out your anger, pulled up the anchor
so your ships of sadness washed upon my shore

You're a monster, devilish creature, lying preacher-
Oh what a load of crap

All my faces

You called me and you caged me
You waited then set the trap

I lay here, upon this altar
but to you I am no God
From the beginning,
it was all
a
lie

Jasmijn Muijser

39 Your father's son

You lied
You lied
You lied to me

To love, to keep, we weren't meant to be

Your rogue allure
was what pulled me in
Should have realised you were just lonely and sad
All the lies you spilled, with love-bombing distilled

It's funny now I see it, it makes me so mad
That false sense of godhood you act on
You'll always deny it
but *you really are your father's son*

40 Madness

I long for you
the way I do for madness
I shouldn't
and yet
I do

41 Creativity

Felt so uninspired for a while
I thought I lost myself
My artistic flow, my prose
They say diamonds are created under pressure
it just turned me morose

But now the days look brighter
When found again creativity glimmers
Once she comes to me, I invite her
to inspire, I am the writer
in blood and bones, can't deny her
She's a flood of words, the queen of swords
Once merged, I revel in her rebellion
she changes me for the better

If I have to beg
to keep her I will
I know I have a purpose to fulfil
So I fall
to my knees

All my faces

willing

to pay

all fees

For I do not exist without my words

42 No Man's Land

All my life
I've known bullies
Turns out religious ones are the worst
They exclaim not to exclude
yet a woman is either a slut or a prude
Tell me what it is, this impossible paradox
How do I win this game
and not get drowned with the rocks?

There's a conflict of interest
a holy war
I'm torn between ego and spirit
What do I do?
Know the who's who?
Scrape my knees up
all this damage I can't undo
Then arrives a messiah
he makes me sign a prenup
not to spill on these patriarchal lies
or any other schemes, their victims' butchered cries

All my faces

He promises my soul to be golden
purged from all these good riddance sins

Gave religion the finger
Haven't seen that Man since

I put up with this hate, these witch hunts
Bitter men groaning bitter grunts
I'm done with this bowing, endless broken vowing
I've made friends with the curse
how can it possibly get worse?

This is no place for God's hand
my body, my decision
I am a No Man's Land

Jasmijn Muijser

43 Poet sickness

Perhaps,
by some deformity
it is the mind of a poet
who suffers most

44 My body became my graveyard

There's a part of me
always hiding
behind such a courageous front
The smart girl, mind-reader
The gifted child, age-speeder
(I was never real)
Playground cheater
Hated girl

Lost myself in the war
Brittle soldier, lifted the bar
too high, somewhere I fell down
lost my wings, broke the ice
I nearly drowned

Wise girl, born from nothing
had to claw my way out
of Death's grip
My body became my graveyard
lost all for nothing
no matter how much I gave

45 Social media ruined my life

I've always been
so easily influenced
by the dreams and beliefs of others
The urge to follow those
so hurriedly
or else I'll never be good enough

46 Concrete capitalism

A poet once told me
that to make art is to love truly
and that everything about our bodies
is political

Isn't it sad?
This race we live in
The sheer beauty of this earth
condensed by black smoke
and concrete, capitalist skyscrapers

I long for the day
where I can unravel my anxiety
and unpack the productivity beast
that tells me I should keep working
proving I am *worthy* of a life

Jasmijn Muijser

47 A song in orange

Art comes
when it's not forced to
When I let go
and enjoy the smallest of things
A tired bee I placed upon a flower
the crinkling of candy papers
in the back of my father's car

Creativity is a song I see in orange
vibrant tones the muse whispers to me
When I feel her I am happy
the most comfortable in my skin

But to feel her I am always looking
trying to bleed the words out of me
It is a tiring process
breathing in exhaust gases
with hopes to heal within

Jasmijn Muijser

48 Murphy

I miss you and I'm sorry
for everything
I did and didn't

Do you know
I slept in your bed
when you were gone?
I was a kid couldn't believe it

I still hate
having to let you go
I miss you and I'm not sorry
Why did you have to go?

49 Starvation

I take into account

all of these unsaid wishes

sit down

and mourn

past versions

I shouldn't have been

Little girls with long braids

invigorating dreams

carrying

sleeves of inhuman sadness

Girls who trusted

and wept

Celebrated happy victories

and the demise of her own health

I tasted Death

on the footsteps of starvation

lonely and aching

chillier than it should have been

All my faces

I solaced my weeping father
a little boy who does not cry

All because
my bones stretched my skin
too far, there was nothing
but a skeleton of me
I should have died
but I didn't

To this day I still do not know *how*

Jasmijn Muijser

50 Glitter girl

Glitter stains my lashes
glossy red lips to brave
this foul world

I figure if I just pimp myself
a little brighter, a little cooler
a little bit less like me
I'll be able to hide this shaking
this panic that visits me
even when I sleep

I hide away my dispositions
and the gaps between my age
Guess I should be out partying
although it makes me want to crawl
inside my skin
Gods, don't let them see me
I wish someday I'd really be seen

They all think they want me
but how can they?

All my faces

When this is purely a reflection
of what I know they want to see
I shouldn't leave without passion
though I know I can never
give them peace

When you look upon me
Do you really see me?
A messed up project
A glamorous girl in the works
They admire me for my silence
mystery alluding their aspirations
a show they orchestrated to be

Leave me with my words
the company of all my failures
A thousand faces, the same bloodstained key
Please, keep your opinions to you
Within my words, my madness
if only for a little while
 I get to be *free*

51 Perpetuity

I've never wanted
this life, to grow older
I just want
everything to stay the *same*

52 A girl and her sun

I wonder if it is art

laying here,

makeup done

so consciously

soaking up the sun

53 Flowers

Flowers grow from rotting corpses
I've been dead for a while
how long must I wait

to be beautiful?

54 Obsession

I'll stare into your soul
and make you bleed
your love for me like a purpose
With me you can never sleep

55 Red

Most days
it feels like
there is this hole in my chest
and I'm bleeding
Out
  Out
    Out

I've spent my life
trying
to find a way to close it
I'm still
dripping

R.E.D

56 Boys will be boys

Boys will be boys

Girls will be torn open

by the world

strangers onlooking

hungry gaze

I thought he was friendly

So tell me

why it hurts

stings

burns

when I realise

he has thought

of me in bed

Touched himself

to the idea of me

without

my

consent

How do I get *clean*?

Jasmijn Muijser

57 En pointe

I carry
such agony
embedded into me
like a song

Haunted piano
keys striking
a little rustier
each time
my spine bends
and my chest hollows
When the soil absorbs my tears
I hear the voices
of promises I never kept
The faults in my character
picked raw in performance
by a 19th century audience
that doesn't even know my name

Tell me
say to me what I must do

All my faces

to oil the cracks

and stand

en pointe

to raise my chin to the Old Gods

and thank them

for putting me here

I don't know how

58 A feeling I possess

Open wound
tender heartbreak

Softly,
the rain patters
down my face
Leaking
from a place

that *burns*

59 Validation

I long for words of confirmation
affirmingly etched into my skin
To hear them from people I admire
so for a second I am free
of this tireless pushing
The constant battle to improve myself
my value worth in brilliance
I've always felt I lack

To draw with chalk when it is pouring
to stitch a wound that cannot be closed
perhaps because I have never been outstanding
admired for my beauty or my brain
this academic itch in me is growing
flaring into blue flames

Jasmijn Muijser

60 Was it worth it?

I hope, one day
I can see clearly

Where I've come from
What it was for
So all my soulless nights
have not been for nothing
Burned myself
at the stake of my flaws
Picked myself apart
like it was winter
to feed a town of hungry mouths

I hope, one day
I can ask myself
"Was it worth it?"
and know
it was & was not

61 Dead

I write better
when there's a part of me
that's *dead*

62 Thirteen

When I was thirteen
I starved myself to the bone
Fuel lit with sadness
I thought I was living the dream
Shrinking sizes, organs in crisis
I remember being so alone
Thought it would make me better
easier to love
and for a while it did, gave me such a kick
but then I just got sadder and sadder
There was a hunger in me
an empty, gnawing pit
couldn't walk anymore
so weak I'd only sit
When I was thirteen,
I was barely a person

And even though the mirror showed me
it was the hardest thing
I've ever had to admit

63 Hallways

I see you
in dreams and hallways
our end open ended

Tell me
did you plan this
when we first befriended?

64 Angels

Perhaps it is animals
who bear the wings of angels

Perhaps it is them
to whom this earth belongs

65 Perfectionist's curse

It is my first time living
although I lose touch of that sometimes

When the perfectionism takes over
my mind never stays sober
of the grunts and grits
I should sharpen my wit
Have to do better
Have to be a go-getter

Every day, I think I should know
how to do it all
how to excel like Marilyn Monroe
Every day, I forget
that failing shouldn't make me so upset

-everyone makes mistakes

66 Revelations

I've been having revelations
In the depth of night, white light
reflects off my ceiling- the sight never changes
There's a pit inside me that keeps on growing
I'm a cracked glow stick that
has long stopped glowing
They say people have a limit, a reserve
of how much pain they can take
Well mine's long been overflowing
it's almost like the end of days

I'm the youngest daughter
my lips taste like saltwater
I've been trying my best
to be good, to not show the gaps in me
To fit in with the rest, must always be a step
further- to prove my worth
I must simply be the best
Can never relax, I guess that's the tax
I pay, every morning I patch up my cracks

Jasmijn Muijser

All my faces

Hardly smiling, they only see me fail
never trying
It's funny, I used to be so hailed

I've been having revelations
painful sensations
I guess there must be something
wrong in my
foundation

67 Falling

I'm sure
of everything and nothing alike
perhaps that is the price of living
in its contrast a strike
People always look for what they're missing
to busy fighting what they have
and hold so dearly, only realising its value
when suddenly it is no longer near

Humans are a paradox, I understand that
even though some days I don't get it at all
To climb after the fall, a pitiful gaze
A quick pat on your shoulder
"C'mon now don't linger"
Don't feel your pain, "it's not for winners"

So fall without falling, you have to
develop in life there can be no stalling
Tell me how to figure it out
without telling me *what to do*

Jasmijn Muijser

68 Tortured poet?

Am I a tortured poet?
Am I made to bleed?

Do I cause fear in others?
Does the outside conjure fear in me?

If to love is not to harm
then what was it between you and me?

69 I have never been my age

Bright child
Teacher's pet
I worked so hard to be something
Gave up all my wild
my spark, my wit, my youthful wonder
Like I was already too old
felt like I couldn't feel it, only being sombre

I dream of playing in the sandbox
making mud pies with roses and rocks
they were my favourite now I'm older
But back then I felt so guilty
so ashamed of not growing up colder

Wish so bad I could go back
even just for one day
to get back that pure enjoyment
that free spirited joy I now lack

They say not to be afraid of getting older
but I have always been

Jasmijn Muijser

All my faces

how childishly pathetic that may seem

Because I lost something then
that love for life I've never felt again

70 More than someone's wife

I should burn myself for you
give my life, be your wife

It is the highest order of love, they say
be an object, meaningless trophy, ever on display

Can't be a dreamer, only a ring can redeem her
Can't speak out, can't go out
without being endangered
by strangers, they all want to attain her

Can't be wise, that's only for guys
Shouldn't be so mean, they tell me to give up my dreams
and settle for less, there's no means for success
they just want us to undress
But nonetheless, I digress
I can't help but wanting to express, my distress
and confess that I will never give up my life

I can be more than someone's wife

71 Crisis

Just when I reached my goals
started this commotion
Reject all notions
preconceived- who am I supposed to be?
I wouldn't have put all of this in motion
Please, does anyone have a potion
to ease my mind, I feel like I've been left behind
in life, in a crisis
Not even my mid-life

Don't know what I'm doing
all the questions are queuing
I'm looking for answers, which once again
I *fail* to find

72 Got into uni

I lost all my friends
and I'm running out of breath
on the brink of nineteen
Got into uni, don't know what happened to my dream
Worn to my bones, I can't pick up my phone
I don't want to be seen
I should be excited to learn, can't help but
yearn for quieter times
just me, my pen and my rhymes
Have to dig so deep to get out of bed
don't know if this is normal
I'm hanging on by a thread
All the professors and my parents
they sympathize, but I can hear them think
"It's all just in your head"

Jasmijn Muijser

73 Dropped out of uni

Tried out uni, something new
dreamt of it six years, then in a few days it blew
over and I fell apart
I know intelligence is not the issue-
so why do I feel
so pathetically unsmart?

Feel like I failed,
like once again I bailed
Others don't understand
they just can't comprehend, how wrong
it seemed in my bones
could no longer picture my dream
Passed so many milestones
on the way, blazing to get there
Is this a joke? Am I hazing myself?

I should have been happy
how come my dream has gone rogue?

74 Alcoholic tendencies

Like an alcoholic
turns to the bottle
I turn to my words
when life gets heavy
although with brutal honesty
I know they're there
to patch me up

75 Blue moon rivers

Little girl,
she was told she could not cry
it wasn't brave, her cheeks must stay dry

Little girl,
didn't want to cry
What would it imply?
That she was weak, didn't want to get picked on
by the other children and the guys

Little girl,
couldn't cry for most her life
but once in a blue moon it leaks
from her eyes and she cries
r
i
v
e
r
s

Jasmijn Muijser

76 Right

It's a shame
how much I've cried
Back in high school, every day was a fight
over pride, bitter people always trying
to create sides
Like we aren't the same
no, we're always the ones to blame
I wonder how they aren't ashamed
of themselves and how they acted
but of course, in the course of history
that always gets redacted

They bring ambulances
to our celebrations, claiming our love
is some sick mutation
when we know it's not

All my faces

Why won't they accept us
make such a fuss, of hate
degrade, gay bait, they're uncultured
like vultures descending
They spew nasty comments, condescending

It's a shame, so many of us have been subjected
to that kind of hate, that kind of damage
I fear nothing can undo

And yet despite it all,
we haven't dropped the ball
It's still us, continuing the fight
for our freedom and our rights
It's still us, trying to make it
not only left, but *right*

Jasmijn Muijser

77 The curse of being a girl

Why does being a girl
always feel like losing?
Can't go out
Can't be loud
Can't speak out about the things we want
for ourselves and our bodies
Always decided for us
Don't make such a fuss about
our lack of rights, don't start a fight
about everything that harms us
Misogynist hate so mainstream
lately we can't even dream
about growing tall, they want to keep us
small- not only in our lengths
We're not supposed to express strength or our opinion

Can't go out with friends
predators always on the offend
Not safe at night, there's always such a fright
You're not safe on your own

Jasmijn Muijser

All my faces

down to our bones we're seen
as just an object
Why can't we be just as free
as anybody- who is a man
with all that they can, without fear
no protective gear and sending their location
to the ones they love and those that hope
they come back safely

Maybe put yourself in our shoes
before you choose
how you treat us
And think about your daughters
and your sisters, your mothers and your wives
Because sadly, in this world

our life is not a given

78 Love you more than life

I love you so much
I can't think of you dying
If I do
I might die myself

79 Please remember my name

I scramble these words

in hopes, to convey to you

that I am human

and that I hope

in a thousand years

there will still be

a piece that's left of me

And I

won't

be

forgotten

80 Jasmine

They call me Jasmine
but I am no flower
never felt delicate enough for that name

It is true I wilt and shatter
but never with beauty so it's not the same

And so, I cannot help but wonder
if my name is a promise for the future
or just the cruel mark of Cain?

All my faces

Jasmijn Muijser

ACKNOWLEDGMENTS

Writing this book has felt like such an inhale. A fresh breeze of salty ocean air that came into my life and changed me down to my atoms. I cannot describe it in any other way. But I do know that I have it all thanks to myself, and to the twelve year old version of me that wanted to be a writer more than anything and encouraged me to go follow that dream, no matter how crazy it seemed.

I never really wrote poetry before this book, not with the intent to actually 'do something' with it like with the rest of my stories. I never considered compiling them into a book, let alone have it be the first thing that I publish. But, after a vacation beach walk with my family, looking over at the wild and unruly ocean- the idea of *All my faces* came to me. And I thought, why not?

So, a huge shout out to myself for believing in my dreams and listening to the muse. Because little did I know that this book would be the best thing to ever happen to me.

I also want to thank my sister, for being the first person I showed this book to.

It was the most terrifying thing I've ever done in my life, but reading your notes and your comments was honestly such a delight. Even though I'm quite sure there were a few threats in there, no matter how much you still deny it.

I also want to thank my dad. When I nervously came to you with the question if you wanted to design a book cover for me, you got to work with such dedication- and that really means a lot to me. I know I wasn't the easiest person to design something for, especially because I wanted everything to be perfect. But I'm so happy with how it turned out- so thank you. I couldn't have done this without you.

Thank you mom, for stopping me from throwing my laptop through the wall when I struggled with properly formatting everything- and helping me figure it out. So far, I've come to the realization that writing the book actually *is* the easy part.

Furthermore, I feel like I ought to thank my dogs, for their endless emotional support and cuddles. I love you guys.

That being said, I hope if you read this, *All my faces* came into your life and changed something, just like it did for me.

Love, Jaz

All my faces

Jasmijn Muijser

ABOUT THE AUTHOR

Jasmijn Muijser (or Jaz) -born in 2005- is a poet, writer and animal enthusiast. She lives at home, in the Netherlands, with her parents, her twin and her two dogs. Ever since she was young, her parents called her "een boekenworm" (or bookworm in English) and that has luckily never changed. In her free time, Jasmijn is most likely reading, cuddling with her dogs or crying over cute animal videos, watching Lord of the Rings or Supernatural for the 100th time, drinking too much coffee, buying out the entire thrift store, blasting Taylor Swift's entire discography until her parents get sick of it, or writing in her bedroom slash office. And occasionally she experiences a breakdown due to academic pressure, because she is also studying to get her BA in English.

CONTACT JAZ

Jasmijn is active on social media.

You can find her here:

Instagram @author.jaz

Or you can visit her website:
www.authorjaz.com

In case of inquiries, you can email info@authorjaz.com

All my faces

Jasmijn Muijser

Made in the USA
Las Vegas, NV
14 February 2025

35f98a04-9dd2-4290-825a-f196c3346e7aR01